Your one-two-three step guide to the give-and-take of real-world contract negotiations

by David A. Stone

Second Edition

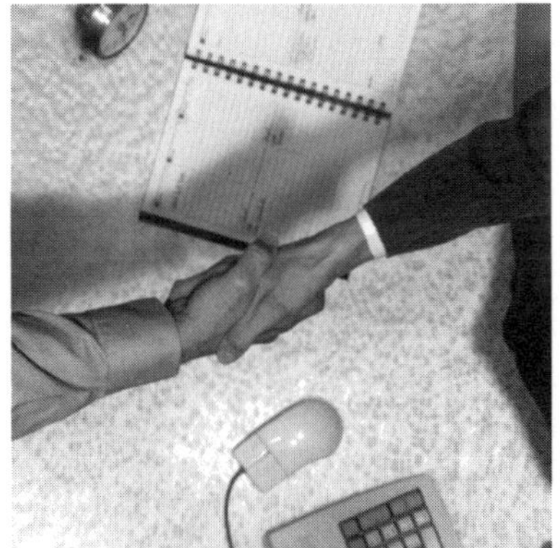

5151 Glenwood Avenue
Raleigh, NC 27612
919.787.8400
919.785-9320 (fax)

ISBN # 0-9648255-6-2

The Negotiation Waltz

Table of Contents

Preface

More often than not, design professionals end up at the short end of a one-sided contract. Why? Because contract negotiation is a learned skill that clients have studied and design professionals have not.

Working to achieve "Win-Win" agreements, this easy-to-read book looks at the essentials of contracts—the good, the bad and the really bad—and the vital skills you need to bring your contract negotiations to a fair conclusion.

You'll study power and who holds it. You'll learn to choose the right negotiating strategy, to properly prepare yourself before the dance begins, to work through each element of the bargaining process—in the right order!

Then you'll get down to the nitty-gritty tactics such as "Good Cop/Bad Cop," "The Flinch," "The Nibble," "Funny Money," and other tactics you need to ensure a fair outcome against skilled negotiators. You need these skills every day. Find them here and put them to work for you today!

Objectives in negotiating

Like Mom always said:
"Learn to get along and
watch out for each other!"

Chapter 1

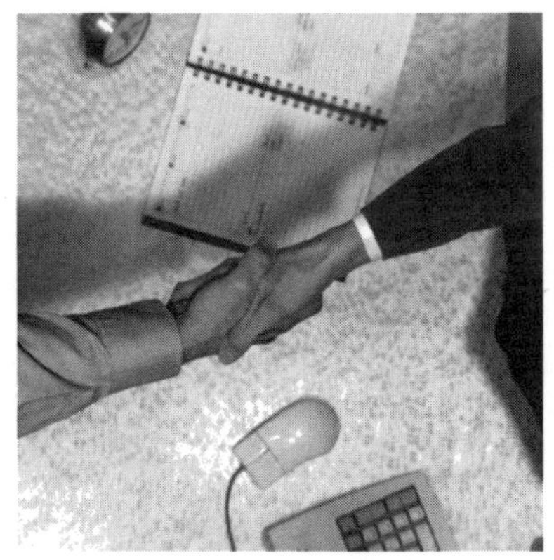

To begin with...

Contract negotiations are a complex undertaking. On the one hand, the goal of formal negotiations is to arrive at a mutually agreeable arrangement that allows both parties to comfortably and enthusiastically begin the project. However, in this business, walking out of the room with a signed contract does not signal the end of the negotiating phase.

The initial negotiation of the contract usually sets the stage and the tone for the ongoing back-and-forth negotiating that inevitably runs throughout the life of the project.

To think that a signed contract document concludes the negotiating phase is to mistake negotiating a design contract with negotiating a deal for a used car.

In fact, these two diverse situations clearly illustrate that there are two kinds of negotiating strategy.

"Deal" negotiating

The negotiating strategy that is perhaps the most common can be referred to as "Deal Negotiating." In these situations the parties are often antagonistic and are looking to walk away from the negotiating table with the biggest share of the pie that they can win.

Key to this strategy is the fact that negotiations typically take place at the end of the relationship and, following negotiations, the parties do, in fact, walk away and the relationship is over. The classic example is the stereotypical deal on the used car lot.

From the moment you walk on the lot the salesperson is your best friend. You have an instant friendship and he thinks your children are the sweetest and best behaved kids he's ever met. As the sales process unfolds this complete stranger grows closer and closer until he's the best buddy you've ever had.

But now you've found a car you like and the serious negotiating begins. He remains your good friend but suddenly he's not quite so willing to do "whatever it takes" for you. As negotiating proceeds, the relationship is cooling and now he'd do anything for you, "if only it weren't for that unreasonable sales manager."

Eventually you reach a deal and sign the papers. At this point you feel the relationship wane quickly. As details are wrapped up, things cool off quickly to where you drive off the lot and the relationship is over.

In a "deal" situation like this, the negotiating happens at the end of the relationship. Once the deal is struck the relationship is over and, since one party has invariably won and the other lost, the parties never care to see each other again.

"Relationship" negotiating

But you're not selling used cars.

In fact, you are selling a complex, long-term service that requires a high level of trust and communication to be successful. Because of their complex nature, design projects require a different approach to negotiating.

In every design project the negotiating happens at the beginning of the project. The purpose of the negotiation is to establish the terms of the relationship that is about to begin.

Most projects are long, complex affairs. Throughout the project the client and the consultant are working closely with each other, often in highly stressful situations, virtually every day for many weeks, months or sometimes even years. Unless the project has been kicked off with a successful negotiation which leaves both parties satisfied and anxious to live up to their end of the agreement, the time together could be agonizing.

Relationship negotiating, at the beginning of a project, seeks to achieve a "win-win" outcome so each party sees the relationship as positive and is motivated to not only fulfill his or her obligations but to actually help the other party achieve their goals.

An agreement built on this type of negotiation establishes the relationship. It sets the stage for the long term association you are entering and it establishes a productive and agreeable dynamic between you and your client. Let's face it. You're going to be in each other's way for a long time. It makes a lot of sense to start off on the right foot.

The key to success in this effort is the ability and willingness to understand each other's concerns and issues. A good relationship *sets up and clarifies each party's expectations.* With these expectations clearly understood on both sides of the table, the potential for disagreement, conflict, and litigation falls off fast.

Sometimes, understanding the other party's issues means knowing that certain terms are just <u>not</u> negotiable. Overhead caps, salary caps, and the invoicing process, for example, may not be open for discussion when you're dealing with certain government agencies. The more you know about the situation in which your clients find themselves, the more you can work with and around their constraints.

Of course ultimately, if you determine you can't live with or make money within their parameters, don't enter the contest. On the other hand, even if some aspects are carved in stone, there are many issues that can remain quite negotiable such as scope, schedule, contract type, etc.

It is extremely important to not get hung up on small issues. Keep the end goal in mind and remember there are many different ways to reach the same outcome.

Underpinnings of relationship negotiating

The basis of any business relationship is that each party has something the other wants. In the case of our friend the car dealer, you want his car, he wants your money. But we have to be careful to not assume that money is always the ultimate goal of a negotiation.

When you learn to listen well and truly understand the other party's concerns and issues, you begin to realize that not everyone wants the same thing.

If the first big lesson is that different people want different things, the second lesson is that price is not always the most important aspect to either or even both parties.

In the case of a design project, there is always a lot more on the table than simply services exchanged for money. There are many aspects to the services you offer which can become negotiable and allow you to arrive at a mutually agreeable contract and a win-win outcome.

Some years back, Mercedes-Benz was looking to capture a larger share of the market in North America. The problem they faced was that, although many people thought it would be nice to own a Mercedes, most of them could not imagine being able to afford one.

At that time the usual car-buying practice was to arrange for a three-year car loan. At the end of three years, the loan would be paid off, the warranty would be over and little (and sometimes big) things would start to go wrong with the car. At that point many people would trade the car in for a new one. The monthly payments on a three-year loan for a Ford or Chevy were within most people's reach, but the payments on a Mercedes were just too high.

The creative thinkers in the Mercedes organization realized that people were less interested in purchase price than they were in the size of their monthly payments. So, instead of financing the car over three years, they built and marketed a program to finance the car over a five-year term.

The program played on Mercedes' legendary quality and reliability and told how a five-year-old Mercedes was in better condition than a three-year-old Ford. Of course—and this is the most important part—financing over such a long period also lowered the monthly payments to a point where more people could afford them. The result? Mercedes' sales rose dramatically, and the finance company (also owned by Mercedes) profited handsomely from the additional interest payments.

Car buyers were less concerned about price than they were about monthly payments. Mercedes side-stepped the price question by offering more attractive terms. By understanding the other party's concerns and issues, they were able to increase car sales without lowering price.

The key here, as in all successful negotiations, is that Mercedes listened carefully, and exercised flexibility in their dealings. If you can learn to understand your clients' concerns, you can have the same kind of negotiating success.

Never narrow it down to just one issue

In a good relationship, both parties walk away winners. They both feel they've made their share of compromises and have been granted their share of concessions. To make your negotiations successful you have an obligation to help the other party feel like he or she has won.

That's worth repeating:

You have an obligation to help the other party feel like he or she has won.

A key success factor in this effort is to never narrow negotiations down to just one issue.

Let's say you've been talking about the project and you've come to agreement on scope, schedule, quality, meeting dates, submittals, and all the details, except price. Everyone is feeling very positive, but you still have to get over the price hurdle. You want one fee and the client wants to pay something less. With price as the only issue left on the table, one of you is going to win and the other will lose. Someone is going to have to make a compromise that they don't wish to. Then, despite all your previous success, either you or your client will walk away feeling defeated.

If, instead, you reached *general agreement* about the previous issues, but left them subject to an agreement on price, you could use one of the other issues to let both parties win. For example, the client is willing to pay you a $35,000 lump sum fee, but you want to hold out for an extra $3,000. In your previous discussions, the client had wanted you to include record drawings in your package. You had negotiated them out, however, anticipating the client would be tough when negotiating money.

To bring the talks to a win-win conclusion, you offer to provide the record drawings if the client would be willing to pay the higher amount. The client agrees and both parties walk away from the table as winners.

How can you tell it's successful?

A good negotiation is a growth process in which both sides learn about each other and are willing to give-and-take to seek a mutual ground from which a project can be accomplished. It's not a battlefield or a competition. It's a compromising and supporting environment from which both sides emerge excited and motivated to do the best job possible for each other.

You can always tell when you've accomplished a win-win outcome in your negotiations because:

1. Both sides feel a sense of accomplishment
2. Both sides feel the other side was fair
3. Each side would like to deal with the other again
4. Both sides leave the bargaining table enthusiastic and motivated to get on with the project and live up to their side of the agreement.

But...

As much as you want to achieve win-win results from your relationship negotiating efforts, there are two important concepts to understand:

1. Not everyone you will be dealing with buys into the win-win concept.

Part of your ongoing effort is to find the right clients, whose approach to business dealings is compatible with yours. You want clients who also believe that win-win is the right outcome.

Along the way you will invariably (and sometimes frequently) encounter those who bring a different philosophy to the bargaining table. In their view, win-win means they win twice. They are looking to extract every concession possible. They have little or no concern about a long-term relationship or your ability to sustain a viable business.

Sometimes a win-win outcome requires that you stand up and vigorously defend what is rightfully yours. To do this, you have to learn to be comfortable with confrontation and be wary of those who truly are out to get you. There are times when paranoia can be useful!

2. *Win-win negotiating does not mean you become a doormat.*

You achieve a strong and fruitful relationship by standing up for what is rightfully yours while making meaningful concessions that help the client achieve his or her goals. Laying down and saying, "whatever you want is OK with me," is not win-win, it's win-lose. The only difference is, you're volunteering to be the loser!

Design professionals must learn to reach win-win by being equally concerned with what is good for the firm and good for the client. This means guarding against a growing scope of work over the life of the project, acting quickly when unpaid receivables grow too large or too old, and pushing hard to limit your liability to a reasonable level.

Win-win means just that -- you both walk away feeling you have been treated fairly.

Progress Review: Part 1

Check either True or False in response to each of the following statements.

True False

❐ ❐ 1. A good negotiation sets the tone for the entire, long term relationship of the project.

❐ ❐ 2. Doing business with good friends is the most important key to success in "deal" negotiating.

❐ ❐ 3. The long-term, complex nature of design projects makes it important to begin with a solid relationship.

❐ ❐ 4. A good relationship-type negotiation sets up and clarifies each party's expectations.

❐ ❐ 5. Ultimately, every project negotiation boils down to a contest over price.

❐ ❐ 6. Careful listening and flexibility in dealings can overcome almost any sticking point in a negotiation.

❐ ❐ 7. The client is responsble for looking after themselves and protecting their own interests in a negotiation.

❐ ❐ 8. It's a good idea to go through your negotiating items in checklist fashion and settle them one at a time.

❐ ❐ 9. You can tell you've accomplished a win-win in your negotiations if both sides feel the other side was fair.

❐ ❐ 10. As much as you desire a win-win outcome, you can't always count on the other party to want one too.

Score your responses

1. - T 2. - F 3. - T 4. - T 5. - F
6. - T 7. - F 8. - F 9. - T 10. - T

9 - 10	Great	You clearly understand the objectives in a design firm negotiation.
7 - 8	Good	A quick review would be helpful before you sit down at the bargaining table.
0 - 6	Poor	Hello? Don't negotiate anything until you've gone over this section again.

Preparing for negotiations

Of course you don't have time to prepare. But you don't have time to lose either.

Chapter 2

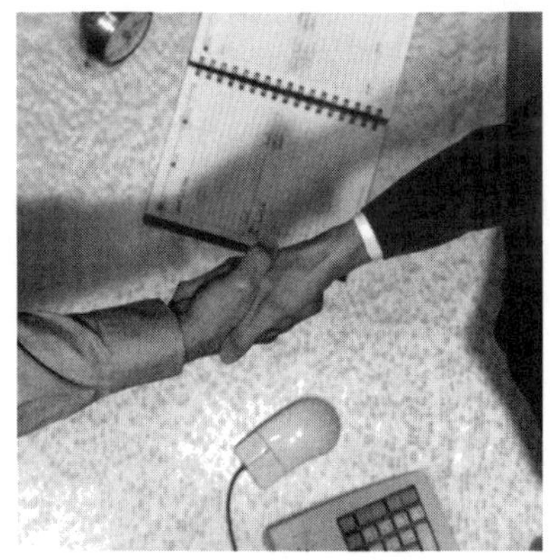

The making of a good negotiator

Negotiation is a business skill. Just as you can be taught to read a financial statement or analyze an investment, you can be taught to negotiate. There are countless negotiating seminars on the market today and even more books and audio and video tapes on the subject.

Your clients are skilled negotiators. If they are in business, they have spent many hours studying and practicing negotiating skills and techniques. They know when and how to make concessions. They can read the other party and tell when a concession is about to be made. They've learned these skills because they understand that negotiating is the highest-paying activity in the business world.

Imagine that you are negotiating a contract. Because you have studied negotiating techniques you spend an extra 30 minutes in discussions and succeed in increasing your firm's fee by $10,000. Where else, except in negotiating, can you earn $20,000 per hour?

Here are a few keys to becoming a successful negotiator.

1. Have a desire to learn and practice negotiating skills.

We've said there is no shortage of sources to learn these skills. Likewise there is no lack of opportunities to practice them. Like any skill, you become better with practice. Every day, at work and in your away-from-work life, you have an endless series of situations in which you are negotiating.

At home with your children; when you're shopping; at work with your boss, your fellow workers, and your subordinates; you are negotiating all the time. By learning negotiating skills, you can practice them every day. When the time comes to negotiate a contract, you'll be much better prepared.

2. Understand negotiating skills.

Many of the skills and techniques of negotiation are based on psychological principles. In order to help your clients achieve what they want, you must be able to understand what they want. While some negotiating techniques can be manipulative, others are simply human nature in practice. When you understand how they work, you'll be much better equipped to use the techniques.

3. Understand that both sides are under pressure.

Many rookie negotiators are under the mistaken notion that the pressure is all on them to make concessions. The reason the other party is at the table is that you have something they need or want. If the negotiation is the conclusion of a long selection process, the client isn't interested in starting all over with someone else. They want the process to succeed. You have significant value to bring to the table, and your client is under just as much pressure to reach agreement as you are.

4. Have a desire to create win-win negotiating situations.

You will become a successful negotiator if your client knows you to be working to achieve a fair and equitable agreement. Your reputation as a fair and reasonable business person will go ahead of you and clients will want to work with you again and again.

Knowing your contract

The contract document you typically use forms the basis of the relationship you have with a client. As such, you, or any of the principals, project managers, or staff who are negotiating or dealing with clients have a need to know and understand that contract. Chances are, however, that many of those people haven't thoroughly read or clearly understood the contents of that document.

Do something to change that right now!

Contract clauses are violated every day and, in many cases, the design firm, not the client, is the main culprit. A lack of understanding of your contract agreement needlessly exposes you to tremendous liability risk. Out of ignorance, you or your staff could be making serious errors or omissions that can lead to reduced profitability in the short term and litigation down the road.

Here's how you can protect yourself.

Plan a series of noontime, "lunch-and-learn" seminars in which you, your corporate counsel, or your insurer review the contract in detail with your staff and project managers. In preparation, have the contract printed out clause by clause so the group can review one at a time.

As a group, examine each clause and discuss it so that everyone develops a clear understanding of what it means in simple English. Many contracts have been written by lawyers using legal jargon which the rest of us can't fathom. The purpose of this exercise is to ensure that you can explain, in your own words, the meaning of the clause.

Next, discuss the reason or reasons the clause was included in the contract. The author of the contract obviously felt the additional effort to be worthwhile, and there would be some legal implications if it were excluded. You need to understand why it was included and what would happen if it were to be amended.

This contract-awareness exercise may take you a number of sessions to work through the entire contract. But, on completion, you, your project managers, and your staff will be prepared for the next round of negotiations and ready to administer the contract accurately and safely.

The top ten sources of leverage

The process of negotiating is influenced significantly by the circumstances in which each party finds him or herself at the time of the bargaining. Your ability to stand up and insist on getting what is rightfully yours can be aided or compromised by the leverage you bring to the table. There are 10 factors which will seriously affect the strength of your position at the bargaining table. You need to know these items so you can accurately assess your bargaining status at the time of the negotiation.

1. Money

How badly do you need the money this project may produce? Just as when you go to a bank for a loan, the less you need it, the more bargaining leverage you enjoy. If you are about to default on a loan or unable to make payroll this Friday, you're not going to be in a good bargaining position.

2. Time

How much of a rush is the client in to get the project underway? How anxious are you to get the cash flowing? If you're in a great rush, the party across the table from you can easily pressure you into signing a less-than-perfect deal. By indicating that you would like to wrap up negotiations quickly, you will likely prompt an offer which is heavily weighted in the other party's favor. When you turn it down, the other party will begin to debate minute details which are meaningless to the contract, but succeed in wasting your time and putting you under additional pressure to sign.

3. Competition

Have you marketed your firm to reduce the perceived competition? Do you have unique capabilities and service offerings which aren't available anywhere else? If the client perceives your firm to be offering services which are no different from those that can be purchased from many firms, you'll have very little bargaining strength. As soon as you insist on a concession which the client is unwilling to make, he or she could threaten to terminate the negotiation and strike a deal with another firm. If, on the other hand, you offer capabilities and benefits which are hard to find, the client is much more likely to agree to your requests.

4. Experience

How many times have you and your team been down this road? With a wealth of experience under your belt, you have a great deal to offer the client. In exchange for the benefits of that experience, they are more likely to be flexible at the bargaining table.

5. Knowledge

How much do you know about the client, the project, the circumstances? If you know little or nothing about the circumstances surrounding the project, it's very difficult to demonstrate significant value during negotiations. If, however, you can show you are sensitive to the political situation, understand the financial implications of the project, can deal with the personalities involved, you will save the client a great deal of aggravation and education of another consultant.

6. Work load

What is your current backlog? How badly do you need this job? Obviously, if you're desperate to find work for staff members who are sitting idle, you're more likely to give away concessions which you may otherwise hold onto.

7. Facts

Do you have cost data, salary surveys, construction cost data, and other evidence to support your negotiating position? If you can back up a fee or schedule proposal with supporting data it's much harder for your client to refuse your request.

8. Preparation

Have you planned and practiced? Is your agenda set and strategized? Walking into a negotiating session without having prepared your priorities, the concessions you are willing to make and the things you simply aren't willing to concede is to guarantee a significant loss. The best negotiators never begin negotiations without ample preparations.

9. Courage

Do you have the courage to stand up to the client and walk out if necessary? Internal fortitude is a key ingredient of a successful negotiation. Despite the fact that you are seeking a win-win outcome, it's often necessary to stand up and defend what is rightfully yours. Be prepared to announce, "it seems we won't be doing business together after all."

10. Appearance

Is your team physically balanced with the client? Do you have the right age, ethnic, and gray-hair mix? Although not impossible, it is very difficult for a young person to negotiate successfully with a group of gray-haired, aged executives. The social and cultural gap is just too large. Getting the right social mix at the bargaining table also helps to cultivate the relationship in its early stages.

The six lists you need before you walk in

Thorough preparation is perhaps the single, most important key to a successful negotiation. Without it, you're shooting from the hip and unsure where you stand at any point in the process. To help you prepare, you must identify the issues which will be on the table and how you're prepared to deal with them.

The best way to do this is to prepare a set of six lists which itemize those things you're prepared to give away and those you insist on keeping.

1. List of things you want from the client.

This should itemize those things you want included in your contract. This should cover fee, scope issues, schedule, payment terms, special indemnification, etc. You know you're not likely to get all these, but this is what you'll ask for.

2. List of things you are not willing to give up.

Among the list of things you want in the contract, there will be some which you simply aren't willing to give up. Some firms, for example, won't do a design project unless they are assigned the construction administration. Others insist on getting a retainer from a client for whom they have never worked before.

3. List of things you are prepared to trade to the client.

What are the things you're willing to give up in exchange for other concessions? Perhaps you are prepared to lower your lump sum fee by two percent. Maybe you would agree to a tighter schedule. You must enter the negotiations prepared to make concessions. Unless you are, you can't expect your client to make concessions to you.

4. List of things you can do for the client which cost you little or nothing but are very valuable to the client.

Here is an opportunity for you to "sweeten the deal" by making additional concessions which the client may not have asked for. For example, you might be prepared to provide the electronic CAD files of the project, attend a public meeting, construct a model, provide a rendering, or develop some preliminary design sketches for the client's next project. (This last one could also be a good opportunity to get a jump start on negotiating the next project without going through the proposal process.)

5. **List of things the client can do for you which cost the client little or nothing but are very valuable to you.**

There are many things clients can provide you which can prove valuable. For example, they could agree to automatically include you on the short list of their next project. They could provide a good reference or an introduction to another client. If the project is out-of-town, they could provide you with office space in their location. They could also agree to pay your invoices more quickly! There are many ways to be compensated in addition to money.

6. **Written criteria which define the point at which you will abandon the attempt to close the deal.**

Not every negotiation ends successfully. There are times when it is in your best interest to walk away and look for another opportunity. Before you step up to the bargaining table, you need to have defined the criteria which will force you to do this. The reason it's so important to consider this ahead of time is that invariably you will get caught up in the excitement and enthusiasm of the negotiations. In that high energy environment, you may find yourself pushed into making more concessions than you wisely should. You don't want to wake up and discover that you should have put a stop to it a long way back. Decide ahead of time the point at which you should walk away. Then, if you get pushed to that point, you can rationally determine the project isn't worth taking.

Researching the project

Earlier in this section we discussed the top ten sources of leverage and discovered one of them was knowledge of the client, the project, and the circumstances surrounding them. This knowledge can prove extremely useful in your negotiations. For example, if you happen to know the company with which you are negotiating has a president who is bottom-line focused, you may offer to lower your fee by showing how some scope items can be eliminated. Likewise, if you know the company has a history of paying late, you may want to insist on a retainer before you start the work.

Use the following checklists to find as much information as possible about the client and the project:

Client information checklist

- How large is the company?
- What is their financial strength?
- Are they expanding? Downsizing?
- Where else are they located?
- What is their corporate culture?
- Who are the decision makers?
- Are they working with any of our competitors?
- What projects?
- Where are the decisions made?
- How well do they know us?
- Have we worked with them in the past?
- Have we submitted proposals to them in the past?
- What was our performance?
- Who was our contact?
- Do they have other, upcoming projects?
- Do we know if the emphasis is on price, quality, service, etc.?
- Is a local office necessary?
- Do they spread the work around?
- Is there potential conflict of interest with other clients?
- Do they pay their bills on time?

You can find a great deal of this information in these places:

- Their web page
- Dun and Bradstreet
- Copy of their Annual Report
- Standard and Poors Index
- Moody's Index
- Library search services
- Industrial directories
- Copies of their brochures
- Past issues of journals
- The Yellow Pages
- Your bank manager
- Client contacts, friends of the client, your friends
- Regulatory agencies
- Their public affairs office
- The Better Business Bureau
- Chambers of Commerce
- Manufacturing representatives
- Their own marketing representatives
- Related trade groups

Primary decision maker and committee member information checklist

- Name?
- Correct title?
- Who are his/her subordinates?
- Personal goals and ambitions?
- Length of tenure?
- Time in present position?
- Position in the organization?
- What is the assistant's name?
- Technical discipline?
- Graduated from?
- Degrees, Licenses?
- Personality style?

- Professional organizations?
- Trade associations?
- Work habits?
- What are his/her ethics?
- What is the dress standard?
- Can they be entertained or accept gifts?
- Marital status? Name of spouse?
- Children? Names and ages?
- Spouse's occupation?
- Political stance?
- Eating/drinking habits?
- Sports/hobbies/recreation?
- Travel interests?
- Social affairs?
- Reading habits?
- Military background?
- Taboo topics?

You can find a great deal of this information in these places:

- Ask directly
- Peers
- Assistant
- Former employees
- Subordinates
- Mutual acquaintances
- Professional organizations
- Who's Who
- Walls and desk in his/her office

Seven steps to negotiating a consulting contract

1. Scope

What is it the client wants done? What are the parameters and limits to the work? What will be included in the work and what will be left out? Until scope is defined, we can't begin to talk about price.

2. Schedule

How quickly does the client want it done? As with dry cleaning and photo finishing, the sooner they want it, the more it's going to cost. Why? Because you will have to drop what you're doing now and rush to get this project done. You can't determine price until you know what the schedule will be.

3. Team

Who will be working on the project? Your best people have high charge-out rates because they are so good. If the client wants them working on the project, the price will have to be adjusted accordingly. If a sports team wants the first-round draft pick, they had better be prepared to pay the price.

4. Risk

What risks are you being asked to assume? In the design industry, risk comes in two forms: financial risk—the client may run off without paying your bill; and liability risk—you may complete this technically complicated project only to get sued. If you are expected to assume risk, you should be compensated for taking that risk.

5. Quality

If you want a Rolls Royce, you have to be prepared to pay for it. If the client's budget says, "Chevy," don't offer a Cadillac. "Lower quality" does not mean shoddy work or mistakes. It means fewer design alternatives, fewer meetings, generic details, etc.

6. Terms

What payment terms is the client offering? If you're being offered 90-day terms and no markup on reimbursable expenses, you'll want to increase your fee to compensate. On the other hand, if the client is willing to pay you a retainer and agrees to pay all invoices in 30 days, you could afford to make other concessions.

7. Price

Only after you have worked through the preceding six issues can you reasonably discuss price. Of course, you don't want to nail down your understanding on the other six issues until you are ready to reach agreement on everything. You must reserve the right to withdraw an offer if your client becomes unreasonable as discussions wind to a close. For example, you may have reached tentative agreement on 45-day payment terms. But, if the client insists on pressing hard on price, you may want to reach final agreement by taking a lower fee in exchange for 30-day terms.

Progress Review: Part 2

Check either True or False in response to each of the following statements.

True	False	
❒	❒	1. Negotiating is simply an exercise in understanding human nature and anyone can do it.
❒	❒	2. Generally, the design consultant is the negotiating party under the most pressure to make concessions.
❒	❒	3. A good project manager is familiar with the language and the implications of every clause in the contract.
❒	❒	4. A client that is anxious to start a project as quickly as possible can put unreasonable pressure on the consultant to sign a one-sided contract.
❒	❒	5. Good preparation will always pay off in any negotiating situation.
❒	❒	6. A good negotiator will know ahead of time those things they are willing to concede and those they will not trade.
❒	❒	7. A knowledge of the inside politics of a client's organization can be useful in negotiations.
❒	❒	8. You must always nail down scope before you begin discussing price.
❒	❒	9. The risk a client asks you to assume can significantly influence other negotiating factors.
❒	❒	10. Favorable payment terms can sometimes allow you more flexibility in price.

Score your responses

1. - F 2. - F 3. - T 4. - F 5. - T
6. - T 7. - T 8. - F 9. - T 10. - T

9 - 10	Great	Your careful preparation will pay off in your negotiating sessions.
7 - 8	Good	You'd do well to review these important concepts one more time.
0 - 6	Poor	You're going to get railroaded into signing a bad deal if you don't study this more carefully.

Common errors in negotiating

A short lesson in shooting yourself in the foot

Chapter 3

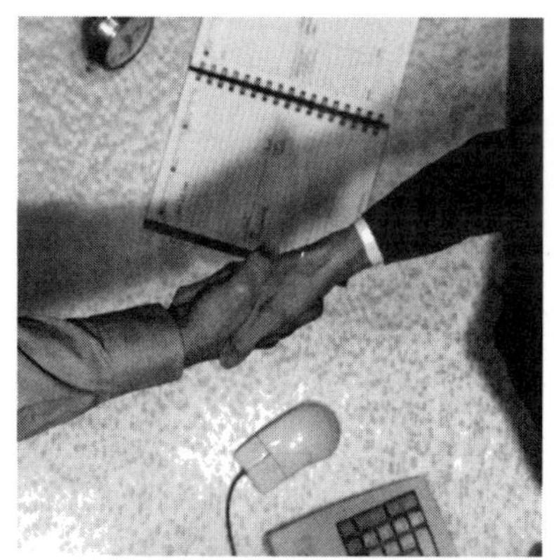

Common errors in negotiating

While it's important to have and use the specific negotiating skills and tactics used around bargaining tables everywhere, it's equally important to avoid the mistakes that are so often made by design consultants.

In studying design firm negotiations, it becomes quickly obvious that there are a series of errors which are made frequently and by many practitioners. As you go through this list, which is in no particular order, be on the lookout for mistakes that you make regularly. Once you are aware of the problem, it becomes easier to correct.

1. Seeing any concession as benefiting one side only

Too many negotiators assume that if the client wins a concession, it's because you lost. As was pointed out in the *Preparing for negotiations* section, each party wants different things. You may want a certain price, but I may be more interested in good terms. By compromising on price to make you happy, I may be able to win the terms I would like.

2. Failing to acquire the skills of negotiation

Bargaining is a skill and many clients are better at it than you are. While you were learning how to design and construct, they were learning how to negotiate. They've had more training. They've had more practice and they clearly understand the benefits of effective negotiation. While it's admirable that you focus your efforts on producing a good project, don't neglect the key business skills that will allow you to still be producing good projects ten years from now.

3. Conceding on fees at the first pressure

For fear of losing the job or in the interest of avoiding confrontation, too many consultants are ready to drop their fee at the least pressure. How many businesses with which you deal as a customer are as willing to lower their price as you? As discussed in the *Preparing for negotiations* section, there are seven issues to be discussed on any design project. Price is just one of them. If you feel forced to make concessions, look elsewhere before you adjust your fee.

4. Treating negotiation as a secondary issue

For too many design professionals, winning the job is most important. We pour our heart and energy into getting the job in the first place and then we lose it all at the negotiating table. Much less energy is put into planning, research, and tactical preparation for negotiating than into the marketing strategy to get the job in the first place.

5. Being unprepared for negotiations

How often have you been in a casual lunch with a client when suddenly you discover yourself answering questions about price and schedule? In cases like this, the client has begun to negotiate and you weren't even aware it was going on. You've had no time to prepare and now you're making commitments you'll come to regret. It's perfectly okay to say, "Let me look at this project in more detail and get back to you with some numbers."

6. Being terrified of negotiating

By seeing yourself as a professional, which in your mind makes you not a business person, you build in a reluctance to get into the nitty-gritty of negotiation with a client. When combined with the natural aversion to confrontation, engineers and architects often work themselves out of the opportunity to negotiate the best deal.

7. Succumbing to market pressure

The law of supply and demand will never be rescinded. If the services you offer are just like those available from many sources, you will have little leverage at the bargaining table. You must ask yourself what it is that truly sets you apart from your competitors. If your services have reached commodity status, you will be under severe economic pressure to take every job, no matter what the fee. Pressure like this puts you into a very weak negotiating position.

8. Relying on old "tariff of fee" habits

For many years the profession relied on a virtually standard schedule of fees. This made life easy since you simply had to look up the fee on a chart. But times have radically changed. First, in many areas, government antitrust legislation has made it illegal for organizations to publish and enforce mandatory schedules. Second, and more importantly, the marketplace for design services has become so competitive that recommended fees have been left by the wayside as clients demand—and firms provide—more services at lower cost.

9. Being perhaps just a little too honest

No one is advocating dishonesty. However, architects and engineers could learn to "keep their cards a little closer to their chests." Far too many negotiations (especially in the public sector) consist of first revealing cost structure, profitability, overhead rates, and any other financial statistic a client cares to review, and only then sitting down to discuss the project. Unless required by statute, your financial data is your private affair. While you may be out to achieve a win-win outcome, you cannot assume that those opposite you at the bargaining table will be as honest as you.

10. Reducing the scope to make the fee work

Every time you accept the client's fee offer and then reduce the scope to fit, you diminish the importance of your role in the project and compromise your ability to deliver the levels of service for which you pride yourself. Many firms today are bemoaning the diminishing role of the design professional. In many cases, it's those very firms who have allowed their influence to be negotiated away through a lack of ability to function aggressively in a free marketplace.

11. Agreeing to negotiate over the telephone

The telephone is the worst negotiating environment for three reasons. First, the initiative lies with the caller and you are often caught unprepared. Second, the calls are usually short in duration and force you into decisions you aren't ready to make. Finally, since you are unable to see body language, gestures, and facial expressions, you lose a significant ability to communicate effectively.

12. Focusing exclusively on fees

In the *Preparing for negotiations* section, price was the last of seven issues on the table when negotiating a design contract. While there's no question that price is important, it can be easily offset by adjustments in terms, risk, schedule, etc.

Progress Review: Part 3

Check either True or False in response to each of the following statements.

True	False	
❐	❐	1. Making any concession in a negotiation simply weakens your side.
❐	❐	2. A good negotiator will work through all the other project variables before giving in on fees.
❐	❐	3. Negotiations should always be considered a top priority before the project can begin.
❐	❐	4. The most important phase of any negotiation is the preparation.
❐	❐	5. Many consulting professionals find they shy away from the potential confrontation which a negotiating situation can bring.
❐	❐	6. It's very easy to submit to the pressure of a client telling you that another firm is willing to offer a lower fee.
❐	❐	7. If you don't want to negotiate, you can always rely on your association for a recommended schedule of fees.
❐	❐	8. Any information about your firm that a client wants to know should be readily given to them.
❐	❐	9. You should not immediately offer to reduce scope to match a client's price offer.
❐	❐	10. Telephone negotiations are convenient and fast for everyone involved.

Score your responses

1. - F 2. - T 3. - T 4. - T 5. - T
6. - T 7. - F 8. - F 9. - T 10. - F

9 - 10	Great	You will likely avoid the most common errors on your way to success.
7 - 8	Good	Run through these again to make sure you don't hurt yourself with mistakes.
0 - 6	Poor	Are you asleep? Maybe you should be negotiating for their side!

Negotiating tactics

Oh, so that's what happened to me on the last project!

Chapter 4

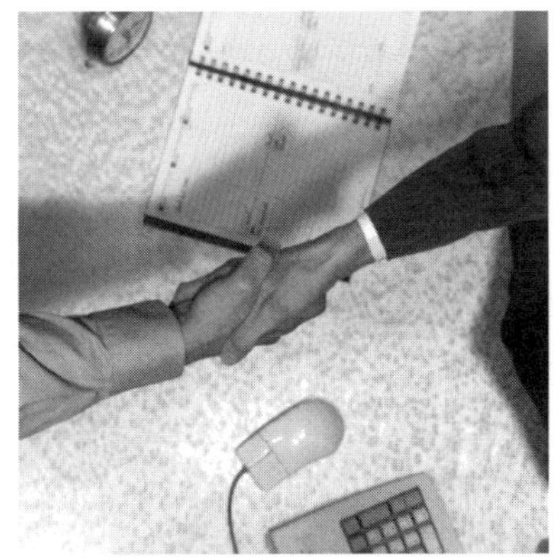

Warning!

As you read through these tactics you'll likely be offended by some of the seemingly "low-down" tricks which can be, and are regularly used in negotiating. You may, in fact, determine that these tactics seem so underhanded you could never envision yourself using them. That's a perfectly valid response.

You must learn about these maneuvers, however, because they are being used against you all the time. You may even see what it was that coerced you into signing that last contract, even though you knew it wasn't right.

Once you're familiar with these tactics, you can recognize when they are being used on you and effectively defend against them.

Negotiating "gambits"

Anyone who has ever been involved in a competitive sport knows there are two levels of knowledge and skill required to be successful. There are the basic, physical skills necessary to play the game well. A baseball player learns to throw and catch the ball correctly. A basketball player learns to dribble and shoot. These fundamental skills are the tools the player uses in every game.

Equally important in preparation is to develop the strategic knowledge of the game: how to react in different situations, how to prepare a game plan to respond to the strengths and weaknesses of an opponent, etc.

Until now we have been discussing the strategic negotiating issues that affect your design contract. Things like scope, schedule, quality, terms, risk, and price are all subject to negotiation and you have worked hard to prepare your arguments and your strategy.

But, just as the tennis player has to master the backhand before he or she can implement a game strategy, you must learn the techniques used to achieve a successful outcome in negotiating.

Just because you would be willing to trade better payment terms for a lower fee and have asked politely, doesn't mean the client won't insist on low fee and payment terms favorable to him or herself. You must use your negotiating skills to persuade the client to make concessions from their side of the table as well.

The skills you will use are often referred to as negotiating "gambits." In the game of chess, a gambit is a move for advantage. In the game of negotiating, it's the same thing. By learning these tactics you not only use them to achieve your desired outcome, you can be aware when they are being used against you and mount an appropriate defense.

Some of the tactics are well known. The "Good Cop/Bad Cop" technique, for example, is an old favorite that appears in every good detective movie. Others are less well known and more subtle.

"Win-win" revisited

Discussions about "devious" tactics like these might seem to be working against the goal of a win-win outcome. You must realize, however, that as much as you want both parties to walk away winners, your future client may not always share your sentiments. There are plenty of business people who would like nothing better than to retain your services at the least possible price under terms and conditions that are decidedly in their favor.

Remember again: win-win does not mean you lie down and offer to be a doormat. Friendly, cooperative agreement to any request they make does not result in both parties being treated fairly.

In order to achieve a win-win outcome, you must vigorously defend your position and use your strength against the strength of your opponent. If your future client is also interested in achieving a fair outcome, the negotiation should be easy. If, however, the client is out to win as many concessions as possible, you must use your strength and your knowledge of negotiating tactics to win the concessions you require and defend against unreasonable demands which would make the contract undesirable.

The "Nibble"

The psychological makeup of human beings makes us curious, but often predictable creatures. One example is that, faced with choices, we often struggle to make a decision. It's difficult to choose one option from another. However, once we've made up our minds, we will go to great lengths to rationalize and defend the decision and convince ourselves it was right. Once we have made the really big decision, it also becomes very easy to make smaller, ancillary decisions.

A good negotiator recognizes this trait and uses it to his or her advantage.

The car salesman will be happy to help you decide to buy the "base model" car because he knows it's easy to add the optional $500 CD player after you've made the $17,000 decision on the car. After all, what's an extra $500 when you've already spent $17,000? If, on the other hand, he started by including the CD player, in your effort to bring the price down, you would likely delete that expensive option.

If you are negotiating a large contract which includes the basic services plus many additional services, the client who is nervous about price, might work hard to remove many of your extra services in order to bring the price down. He or she will negotiate the extras out of the contract and be comfortable purchasing the "base model."

Knowing this, you should begin your discussions with a set of core services which can be expanded, rather than a full set of services which will invariably be scaled back.

Be on the lookout for the "Nibble" being used on you. If you have agreed to a scope of work and a price, watch out for clients who come back asking if you would mind adding a seemingly small scope item. Of course, they expect you will do this without expanding the schedule or the price. They are counting on your sense of fairness and unwillingness to "nickel and dime" the discussions. When you agree to the expanded scope, they will try it again. The requests are always in small, seemingly inconsequential increments, but, when it's all added together, the "scope creep" can become substantial.

The "Hot Potato"

This tactic asks you to solve a problem which rightfully belongs to someone else—usually the client. It typically begins with a bold and unequivocal statement which may sound something like, "let's make it clear from the start, I've only got $20,000 to spend on fees for this project." The discussion then moves quickly forward to list all the services they want for their $20,000.

If you "accept" the "Hot Potato" the client has tossed, you will lie awake all night trying to determine how you're going to provide all those services for such a small fee. When the "Hot Potato" is used successfully, you neglect to ask yourself, "Why is this my problem?"

The goal of the "Hot Potato" is to get you to solve a problem which rightfully belongs to someone else. When you agree, the other person has won and you have lost.

When you walk onto the car lot with a Chevy budget, the salesman doesn't worry himself into an ulcer trying to deliver a Cadillac for your Chevrolet price.

The proper response to a statement like that above, is to say, "Fine, we can work within your budget, but which scope items would you like to remove in order to bring the price down to that level?"

A subtly different approach would be to say, "Fine, we can work within your budget, but let me ask you this. If I could show you how we can increase the quality of the project and substantially decrease operating and maintenance costs, but it would raise the fee to $25,000 would you be interested in listening?" Clients will then respond in one of two ways. They will either say, "Read my lips! I said $20,000 and not a penny more!" Or they will respond, "Yes, I'd be interested in hearing about that." In this case, you know the budget is not as cast-in-stone as they would like you to believe.

The "Red Herring"

As its name implies, the "Red Herring" attempts to use one issue as a diversion in order to win concessions on an altogether different issue. For example, let's say you are negotiating with a client for whom you have previously completed other projects. The most recent project was finished more than a year ago.

Suddenly the subject of your discussion turns to his or her dissatisfaction with the quality of the work and the levels of service on the previous project. This has never been mentioned before but now it seems as if the client is extremely displeased with your services.

Your natural response is to be concerned about the current project. Maybe the client is so upset, the project will be handed to someone else! In self-defense, you quickly offer a significant concession, perhaps lowering the price or adding a substantial scope item. This seems to make the client willing to overlook the shortcomings of the previous project and things go ahead as planned.

You've just been the victim of a "Red Herring." If there were so many problems on the previous project, why is this the first you're hearing about it? Why wasn't the subject mentioned before? The fact is, any problems that may have been on the last project are simply being used as leverage to win concessions on this job.

It's often difficult to recognize a "Red Herring" when it is presented. If an issue catches you off guard and takes you by surprise, chances are it's being used as a diversion. The proper response is to keep the two issues separate. You might say, "We were unaware that you felt this way about the previous project. Since it's obvious there are many issues to be resolved, why don't we arrange a special meeting to go over the outstanding issues on that project?" Your objective is to separate the two issues. Don't let issues in one discussion influence your negotiating position on a separate issue.

The principle of higher authority

A good negotiator will always leave a "back door" through which he or she can easily exit when backed into a corner. This is most easily done by appealing to a higher authority.

The scenario goes something like this. You are negotiating with a client who is pushing hard to win a big concession on price. You make the statement that, "I'm going to have to take this $20,000 offer to the board." (Or the committee, my partners, the review panel, etc.) The more vague the entity to which you must take the proposal, the better. If you claim you have to take the offer to "your boss," the client will rightly conclude he or she is negotiating with the wrong person and ask to speak directly to the decision-maker.

Having taken the offer to "the committee" you then come back to the bargaining table saying, "They were in a really tough mood yesterday and absolutely unwilling to accept anything less than $22,000. If we can come up with that additional $2,000, I'm sure we'll have a deal." This approach lets you be a "friend" as the two of you work to outwit "the committee." It also takes the heat off you as the one who is refusing to grant the concessions.

Of course, your client will also try to use the principle of higher authority on you. To counter this effective technique you should ask at the beginning of the bargaining session whether there is any reason why you might not be able to reach an agreement here today. Clients will likely answer, "No." Then, when they claim to have to take your offer to "the board," you remind them of their statement that there was no reason why you shouldn't be able to reach agreement. This applies a subtle, but important pressure by pointing out their apparent lack of authority and may coax them into working with you to find a solution.

If someone questions your need to go to a higher authority, you simply reply, "I could reach agreement if you were able to lower your demands. But you have gone outside the limits of my authority. If you could drop your insistence on this scope item, or increase the fee you're willing to pay by $2,000, we could sign right now."

The "Set-Aside" technique

A successful negotiation often depends on momentum to keep working through the issues that are on the table. If the session gets hung up on one issue or another, people tend to dig in and reduce their willingness to make concessions on other issues as well. If, on the other hand, the bargaining is rolling along smoothly and quickly, even tough issues are usually settled easily.

If you find your session bogging down over a single issue, try setting it aside for a while and focusing on other issues which you know will be easier to settle. You may even want to reignite the energy by offering a concession of your own, or referring to your six lists (see *Preparing for negotiations*) and offering something that costs you little or nothing but has high value for the client.

Imagine, for example, you are negotiating with a prospective client for whom you have never worked before. Because you have concerns about this client's payment habits, you insist on a retainer prior to starting work. The client is equally adamant about paying only after work has begun. The negotiation seems bogged down on this issue, but you do want the project. You suggest that this issue be set aside for the moment, and to show your commitment, you offer to provide assistance with the client's marketing effort by providing a rendering within your lump sum agreement. The client accepts your offer, several other issues are settled and you reach agreement on your request for a retainer.

By restoring the momentum to the negotiating session and showing your willingness to compromise, you can avoid the impasse that might otherwise derail a successful project.

"Good Cop/Bad Cop"

The scene has been repeated countless times. Two detectives are interrogating a prisoner in the police station. One cop is positively brutal in his questioning and is ready to hang the suspect right there and then. Mysteriously, he is called out of the room. His partner, who has been objecting to this heavy-handed approach, takes over with a quiet, soothing tone and apologizes for her colleague's approach. She offers the prisoner a cigarette and some coffee and quietly asks, "we only want to know who was in with you on the robbery."

By highlighting the contrast between the brutal cop and the nice cop, she gets the prisoner to relax and offer information he would otherwise have kept quiet about.

The same technique has been used for just as long in negotiating. One negotiator is arrogant, demanding, and unreasonable. When he gets called away, his partner, who claims to feel the other's demands are preposterous, is as sweet as honey claiming if "we can only come up with another $2,000," she is sure she can get her partner to go along with it. Suddenly she is on your side! Or at least appears to be. The fact is, the two have carefully orchestrated the scene to get you to agree to a concession.

There are two ways to counter this tactic. The first is to point out that you recognize what they're doing. "You're not going to use "Good Cop/Bad Cop" on me, are you? I'm certain your organization would not approve of tactics like that." Simply pointing out that you are aware of the tactic usually takes the wind out of their sails.

The second way to counter the tactic is to let them know that you intend to make no differentiation between who is making the statements. "Everything that one of you says, I will attribute to both of you. Any tactic that one of you uses, I will ascribe to both of you." This way, you remove their ability to work against you from both sides.

"Good Cop/Bad Cop" has been around so long that everyone knows about it. But it's still used because it still works. Be on the lookout for "Good Cop/Bad Cop" and be ready to counter this notorious tactic.

The "Flinch"

The "Flinch" is one of the easiest and most effective negotiating tactics in your collection. It consists of a visible, even flamboyant, reaction to a statement or offer someone else has made. For example, you might offer to provide your client with a fee of $20,000. Your client stands up, slaps his hand against his head and shouts, "Twenty-thousand dollars? You must be out of your mind!"

Human nature immediately puts you on the defensive. Your client is angry and you're concerned the project may go to someone else. Your first reaction is to try to appease them and the easiest way to do that is change your offer. You quickly back-pedal and suggest that you might be willing to do the work for $18,000.

The result? In exchange for a self-inflicted slap on the forehead and an impressive display of overreaction, the client just saved $2,000! And you paid for it!

The "Flinch" is easy, it simply calls for you to be flamboyant and willing to initiate a little confrontation. Unfortunately, most design professionals will go to great lengths to avoid confrontation and are not only unwilling to use the "Flinch," they fall victim to it on a regular basis.

There are two counters you can use to the "Flinch." First, you can simply ignore it. Your opponent jumps up from the table and just about falls over in feigned reaction to your $20,000 offer. Instead of responding to the "Flinch" you carry on as if you haven't heard anything. "Yes, $20,000. And you may want to sign this deal quickly because my partners aren't happy that I've offered you such a low fee! If you leave it too long, they may change their minds."

The second defense against the "Flinch" requires a little more nerve. It calls for you to identify the tactic for what it is. When the client flinches, you respond with, "Nice flinch! Where did you learn to do that so well? I've been working on mine, but I'm not nearly as good at it as you are." Use your discretion on this one since certain personalities may not react well to this tactic.

The "Flinch" is easy, cost-free, and effective. Get into the habit of using it in all your negotiations.

Withdrawing an offer

When you are bargaining with a skilled negotiator, he or she will often try to use the three-year-old child-tested technique of grinding you down. Each time you make a concession, he or she comes back asking for more. This is tiring and frustrating at best. In order to stop the grinding away process, you may have to withdraw an offer which you have previously made.

Let's say you are negotiating fees and you have offered $50,000 and the client wants you to come down to $45,000. You can apply the "resort to higher authority" technique and come back with a statement something like, "Boy, am I embarrassed! Yesterday I told you we could do the project for $50,000. Last night, we went back over the numbers and discovered we can't do it for anything less than $52,000. We feel very bad about this, but we have no choice but to raise the fee."

Your client won't have any of this, of course, and is quick to let you know. "$52,000 is out of the question. Yesterday you offered me $50,000 and we won't pay a penny more!" Suddenly, the $45,000 they were seeking is forgotten and you have successfully stopped the grinding away process.

Splitting the difference

When a negotiation is drawing to a close and there are only small differences between your position and your client's, a common solution is to split the difference. The client has demanded a schedule of 15 weeks, you are asking for 17. The two of you agree to a 16 week schedule and the contract is ready to sign. This approach offers a classic win-win solution.

Be careful, however, of the shrewd negotiator who takes advantage of your offer to split the difference. Here's how the trick works. The negotiation has dragged on for a long time and you are becoming frustrated with the lack of progress. The client is complaining about how long it is taking to reach agreement and you sense he is getting annoyed with you. You are asking for a $65,000 fee and he is insisting on $60,000. The client continually complains about the amount of time you've invested in the project and how it would be a shame to have it come undone when you are only $5,000 apart.

Being interested in creating a win-win outcome, you offer to split the difference. The client says, "You're saying you'd be willing to reduce your fee to $62,500. That's great! Now we're only $2,500 apart and it would be a shame to have it come undone when we are only $2,500 apart." Your offer to reduce the fee has been accepted, but he hasn't agreed to increase his offer in return!

The lesson here is that you should never be the first to offer to split the difference. Try to get the other person to make the offer and you can reciprocate. If you must make the offer first, be sure it's conditional upon their responding in kind.

"You'll just have to do better"

The psychology behind this tactic is similar to that which makes the "Flinch" work so well. It attempts to put you on the defensive and feel forced to come up with a better offer. It's a favorite of school teachers and college professors who are pressed for time. It works like this. Someone makes you an offer and you simply reply, "I'm sorry, you'll have to do better than that." And then you sit quietly. The other person, who now clearly understands that you're not happy, is left to scramble to come up with something better.

Teachers have used this tactic when grading papers. Instead of going to the effort of reading the paper, they will simply write, "You'll have to do better than this" on the front page and hand it back. Invariably, the paper comes back improved at which point the teacher reads and marks it.

If someone attempts to use this tactic on you, your proper response is, "Exactly how much better will I have to do?" This tosses the ball back into the other court and puts the pressure on your opponent to define a price or condition that would be acceptable. The last thing you want to do is to be negotiating against yourself by improving your offer without some way of knowing what is going to be acceptable.

"Funny Money"

A recent radio advertisement for a car dealer offered what seemed like a fabulous deal which they called, "Five to Drive." You were invited to come to the dealership, put five dollars down on a car, and have payments of only five dollars per day! This was an arrangement anyone could afford!

The deal seemed so good because it was expressed in terms of "Funny Money." Normally, when you think about purchasing a car, the numbers which are churning about in your head involve tens of thousands of dollars. Suddenly you were being offered a car in dollar terms which wouldn't pay for lunch.

When you read the fine print and did the arithmetic you discovered that the vehicle was a stripped down, base model of a subcompact, the actual purchase price was over $15,000, monthly payments were $150, the term of the loan was five years, and the interest rate was far higher than was available elsewhere.

The dealer was very smart, however, to express the deal in "Funny Money" because it made the deal seem very attractive and disguised the actual cost. "Funny Money" is used extensively in negotiations for the same reason. Your client may be reluctant to pay you the additional $5,000 of fee that you're asking for. You could phrase your request like this: "Do you realize that you are delaying the start of this project by arguing over less than half a cent per square foot per year over the life of the facility?" Expressed like this, the amount seems trivial. In real dollars, however, it is substantial.

In negotiating, you might try using "Funny Money" to your advantage. If it's used on you, however, always convert it to real dollars.

Emotion

One of the most difficult aspects of any negotiation is to overcome the challenge of an emotional opponent. It's difficult enough to hold your own ground with an easy client. But when someone starts yelling and pounding their fist on the table your challenge multiplies a hundredfold. It's almost impossible to ignore what seems to be a personal attack.

In any negotiation you must always remember that only one thing affects the quality of the contract you will eventually sign. That is the exchange of concessions back and forth across the table. Like all the tactics discussed so far, emotional outbursts are simply another way of influencing that exchange. If you let the intensity of the situation get to you, you will lose in the negotiation.

If a client chooses to get emotional (and always remember, they are choosing this tactic, the emotion is not involuntary) you have three choices. You can simply ignore the emotion and carry on with the discussion of concessions, you can respond with your own, carefully contrived emotional outburst (this requires a judgment call based on the personality of your client), or you can suggest the client is too upset to continue and that perhaps you should reconvene tomorrow to conclude the discussions. In all cases, you have signaled that the emotion has no effect on you and you intend to remain focused on the issues on the table.

How to make concessions

As discussed in Chapter 2, *Preparing for negotiations*, you must enter your negotiation prepared to make concessions. Regardless of how good the deal you offer is, if you make no compromises, your client will feel he or she has lost in the bargaining. The win-win you are seeking will be missed and the relationship will be less than ideal.

The problem with making concessions, however, is that negotiators, like children, have their behavior reinforced by positive results. If they are using a particular tactic and you agree to make a concession, they will conclude the technique works and try it again. The grinding away process will continue until they conclude that no more concessions are forthcoming. Your pattern of concession-making can signal that you won't put up with the grinding-away process.

Let's say you enter the bargaining prepared to reduce your fee by $2,500. You determine the time is right to make a concession and you offer a reduction of $500. The client, rewarded for his or her efforts, tries again and you reduce the fee by another $500. So far, the client sees no reason to stop asking for greater reductions. When you have used up your $2,500 in $500 increments, it will be very difficult to convince him or her that the end is at hand.

Instead, you can signal your position by granting the concessions in a different manner. When you conclude you are ready to make the first concession, make it a good one. Instead of $500, make it $1,500. The client will be very pleased with your generosity and will, of course, try again. The next time though, your fee will drop only $250—a considerable decrease on the return for the effort. The third concession may only be $50. By this time, the client has the clear message that there is no more value in trying to win further fee reductions and will stop trying.

Summary

In the first chapter, *Objectives in negotiating*, it was stated that negotiation is not a battlefield or a competition, it's a learning process in which both sides learn to accept and compromise and to seek a mutual ground from which a project can be accomplished. Unfortunately, not all clients you deal with see things this way.

Your goal is a win-win outcome but your client may have something different in mind. While the tactics discussed here may seem devious at times, you have to use your strength and negotiating ability to reach your win-win target, hold on to what is rightfully yours, and ensure the client is treated fairly as well. A good negotiator understands that strength against strength will bring both parties to a successful and mutually agreeable conclusion. Taking the role of the doormat and agreeing to anything the other party asks for is not win-win.

These are a few of the countless "gambits" used by skilled negotiators. Each one has many variations. Good bargainers will mix and match them creatively to achieve the goal they have set for themselves.

It's likely you will have trouble with some of these tactics. You might even decide you can't bring yourself to use certain ones. However, know that they are being used against you all the time. Be prepared and you can achieve the win-win outcome that a good relationship requires.

Closing the negotiation

In the second chapter, *Preparing for negotiations*, seven issues were identified which are up for bargaining in any design project. While discussions are ongoing, all seven of these "juggling balls" are in the air. While you may reach tentative agreement on any of them, you must not reach final agreement until they are all ready to be concluded. This allows you and your potential client to each make a final concession on different issues in order to achieve a win-win outcome.

Until the time when all seven issues are ready to be concluded, you want to retain the "need" to refer to the "higher authority" which was discussed earlier. However, as soon as all issues are ready to be settled, the person at the table must have full signing authority and be prepared to conclude the deal at once.

Without the ability to sign on the spot, you leave your client open to reconsideration. He or she may come back at the signing asking for "just one more thing."

When the issues have been resolved, sign the contract! Don't wait to have it retyped and cleaned up, sign it immediately. As long as they have been initialed, the footnotes and side-bar edits are all legal. Don't worry if it's not "pretty," since, in most cases where a win-win has been achieved, once the contract is signed, it's put in the drawer and seldom used again.

If you feel the terms are satisfactory and want to bring the discussions to a close, you can offer a final concession to persuade the client to sign right now. You might go back to your six lists and offer to make one last concession "if we can get this thing signed now." Often, this is enough to conclude the deal and let everyone get on with the job.

Progress Review: Part 4

Check either True or False in response to each of the following statements.

True	False	
❒	❒	1. You only need to know these negotiating tactics if you can imagine yourself using them.
❒	❒	2. A win-win situation means the client will happily agree to everything you request.
❒	❒	3. It's your responsiblity to find a way to accommodate a client with a budget that won't pay for the scope.
❒	❒	4. In a negotiation, it is often useful to have to step away to confer with your partners or some other "authority."
❒	❒	5. "Good Cop/Bad Cop" is so well known, it is no longer an effective technique.
❒	❒	6. A strong, visible reaction to a proposal your opponent has made, will often trigger a concession.
❒	❒	7. While splitting the difference is a time-honored way to conclude a negotiation, you must watch out for the shrewd bargainer who will take advantage.
❒	❒	8. You should always beware of dollar amounts expressed in terms like, "per square foot," "per month," etc.
❒	❒	9. When making a concession, make the first one substantial.
❒	❒	10. Always give you and the client a day or so to think over the deal before you sign the final contract.

Score your responses

1. - F 2. - F 3. - F 4. - T 5. - T
6. - T 7. - T 8. - T 9. - T 10. - F

9 - 10	Great	You're on to most of the tricks that can be used to gain an unfair advantage over you.
7 - 8	Good	You should review these again or you may find yourself victim to a shrewd bargainer.
0 - 6	Poor	Stay away from the bargaining table! We can't afford to sign a contract you've negotiated.

Contract options

The right contract in the right place at the right time to serve the right purpose.

Chapter 5

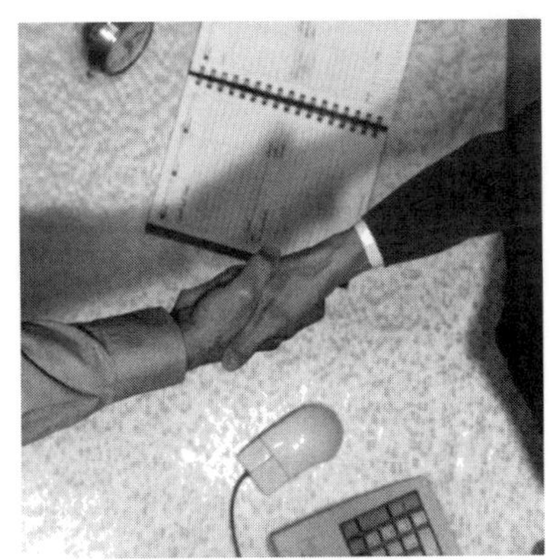

Introduction

Notwithstanding that the basis of all your client dealings ought to be the quality of your personal relationships, the legal basis of your client dealings are the contracts you sign. Too many firms become caught up in the "hunt" to win projects. Then, after the project has been awarded, they focus on the exciting push to complete those projects. In their haste, they often neglect to pay close attention to the vital "rules of the game" which is embodied in the contracts they sign.

Before you even begin to consider the specific terms of a contract, there are vast differences between the contract types available. Each contract type offers advantages in the right situation. On the other hand, each contract type could prove disastrous under the wrong circumstances.

There are two main contract types

1. Value-based contracts
2. Cost-based contracts

Mixing and matching the main features of these two types results in four contract groups of which you should be aware.

1. Value-based contracts
2. Middle-of-the-road contracts
3. Cost-based contracts
4. "Why-don't-you-just-shoot-me-now" contracts

Value-based contracts

As the name implies, value-based contracts are determined and negotiated on the perceived value which you bring to a client. Instead of being calculated as some multiple of the cost you incur to complete the project, the contract identifies an amount the client is willing to pay to "make the problem go away." Your costs, while often being used in initial calculations, ultimately have no bearing on the fee you will receive. Your fee is a reflection of the value clients perceive they are receiving from the work.

There are several examples of value-based contracts, some commonly used and others less well-known.

Value-based, lump sum contracts

The lump sum (or stipulated sum, or fixed-fee, they all mean the same) contract is very simple. Having reviewed and clarified the scope of work to be done, you agree to perform the work for a fixed dollar amount. Once the amount is determined and the contract signed, you are obliged to deliver the services for that amount. If, in the delivery of those services, your costs run higher than anticipated, you could lose some, or even a great deal of, money. If, on the other hand, you have planned well and manage the project carefully, you could complete the project for less than anticipated and make an increased profit.

Payment on a lump sum contract is tied to your performance which provides the firm with a strong incentive to work aggressively on behalf of the client. If the work does not meet preset quality standards, the client has the right to withhold final payment or even ask for the return of some progress payments.

With a lump sum contract, the client enjoys the advantage of a price which is fixed from the beginning of the project and won't change unless the scope is changed. The client assumes little or no risk.

You, too, have significant advantages with a lump sum agreement. The biggest advantage is the opportunity for high profits since the fee is fixed, but you are free to control your costs. On a properly priced and well-managed project, the costs can be considerably less than the fee. Historically, firms which rely heavily on lump sum agreements realize higher profits than those working on an hourly basis. Of course, you must also live with the potential for loss which comes with lump sum. This is a classic example of the "no risk, no reward" maxim. It is ill-advised to use a lump sum agreement if the project does not have a well-defined scope of work.

Summary of Lump Sum Contracts

advantage	Strong advantages to client
advantage	Firm has incentive to do well on behalf of client
advantage	Opportunity for high profit
advantage	Win-win outcome
disadvantage	Risk of loss if project is not scoped or managed well

Value-based, incentive contracts

There are a number of forms which incentive-based contracts can take. These include royalties, in which the firm is paid a percentage of income, profits or savings; equity position, in which the firm is given ownership shares in the project; and incentive bonuses, in which the firm is offered specific monetary rewards for achieving certain schedule or cost control goals.

In one instance, a firm, retained to renegotiate a contract on behalf of a client, turned down the opportunity to be paid a percentage of the savings they would negotiate. Opting instead for an hourly rate contract, they were paid $150 per hour for 100 hours of work for a total of $15,000. Had they chosen to accept the risk/reward basis of the percentage, they could have been paid one percent of the $5 million savings they eventually negotiated for the client — a fee of $50,000 for the same work!

Incentive-based fees also include a significant risk factor since you must be certain of your ability to achieve the goals to which the incentives are tied. Avoid an incentive-based contract if there are circumstances in which the achievement of the goal is controlled by someone else. For example, an incentive is offered for you to achieve a certain project schedule. However, a significant portion of that schedule is used for review by public agencies. Since you can't control the time they take for review, you should turn down the opportunity and use a different contract basis.

Summary of Incentive-Based Contracts

advantage	Client pays fee from savings or profits
advantage	Firm has strong incentive to do well for client
advantage	Strong opportunity for high profit
advantage	Win-win
disadvantage	Risk of reduced profit or even loss if performance goals are not met
disadvantage	Fee revenue and profit are unknown until project is complete
disadvantage	Potential that others could control your ability to achieve goals

Value-based, cost-plus-fixed fee

There is much confusion over the use of the term "fixed fee." When the term is used as a synonym for "lump sum" contract, it refers to the entire fee a firm is paid for a project including labor, overhead, direct costs, and profit. When the term is used in the context of "cost-plus-fixed-fee," it refers only to the amount paid to a firm in addition to the actual project costs (labor, overhead, and direct costs) that firm incurs. In this case, "fixed fee" may end up being your "profit."

In this contract type the consultant is reimbursed for all project costs and then, in addition, paid a predetermined fee. This reduces the risk of many value-based contracts while still retaining the (somewhat reduced) rewards.

Under a cost-plus-fixed fee agreement, clients do not enjoy the same cost guarantees as they do under a lump sum contract, but they do know they will pay only what the project costs, plus the predetermined fee. This will remove any discomfort at the prospect of the consultant making an unacceptably high profit.

The advantage of this type of contract to you is reduced risk. Since the client has agreed to pay all project costs, your risk of loss is eliminated. Of course, as potential risk is limited, so is potential reward. You are guaranteed a profit on the job and that amount is determined from the start. However, regardless of how well or how hard you work on the project, you cannot increase the dollar amount of that profit. Keeping project costs low will increase the percentage of profit you make, but it will not increase the dollar value.

You have an incentive to work in the client's best interest since your ability to control project costs can result in a higher percentage profit. For example, a client has agreed to cover all your labor, overhead, and direct costs for the project plus a "fixed fee" of $5,000. If you take six weeks to complete the project and the client pays $50,000 in costs, your "profit" is 10%. If, however, you manage to complete the project in five weeks and the client costs are $40,000, your profit rises to 12.5%. In addition, you have an additional week in which you can work on other projects and earn additional profit.

Your ability to control project costs will also result in a high level of client satisfaction.

Summary of Cost-Plus-Fixed Fee Contracts

advantage	Firm has guaranteed profit from fixed fee
advantage	Client knows they are paying only for actual project costs
advantage	Firm has incentive to do well for client
advantage	Firm can increase percentage profit by reducing project costs
disadvantage	Total profit dollars cannot be increased
disadvantage	Client does not enjoy cost guarantees

Middle-of-the-road contracts

Middle-of-the-road contracts combine features of both value- and cost-based contracts. In doing so, they offer fewer high-reward advantages and fewer of the inherent risks of value-based contracts.

Middle-of-the-road, percentage-of-construction cost contracts

The percentage of construction contract has been a mainstay of the industry for decades. Using value-based logic, it prescribes a fee based on the cost of construction on the assumption that a more expensive project will require more involvement on the part of the consultant.

The fee is initially calculated on the basis of a construction cost estimate. Once the estimate has been prepared, the fee is converted to a lump sum with all its accompanying risks and rewards. In some cases, the actual construction cost won't be determined until final bids are received. In these cases, the firm's ultimate compensation will be unknown until the construction cost is set. If construction costs end up being less than initially estimated, the firm could be faced with a lower fee than originally expected.

If design and documentation take place in a strong economic period, the fee estimate will be based on a high construction cost. If the economy falters and construction activity slows prior to the project being bid, the actual bid prices could come in significantly lower than estimates. This, in no way, decreases the amount or value of the work the consultant performs, but it does reduce the fee the firm is paid for the contract administration portion of the work.

While this contract type offers straightforward calculation and some value-based features, it has a significant potential for conflict of interest. If the fee is tied to the cost of construction, a consultant could be tempted to increase his or her revenue and profit by driving construction costs up. This is obviously not in the client's best interest. If, on the other hand, the architect or engineer works hard on behalf of the client and succeeds in keeping construction costs down, his or her reward is lower revenue and profit!

Summary of Percentage of Construction

advantage	Converts to value-based contract
advantage	Logically based on size of project
disadvantage	Perceived disincentive to work in client's best interest
disadvantage	If construction costs decrease, fees are artificially dropped

Negotiating percentage-of-construction

If a client asks you to commit to a fee based on percentage of construction, suggest that you will agree to this contract type only if the contractor is willing to guarantee his total cost as a multiple of your fee. If, for example, your fee is to be five percent of estimated construction cost, the contractor's total invoice should be set as 20 times your fee. Of course, no contractor would be foolish enough to agree to such speculation. If they shouldn't, why should you?

Middle-of-the-road, time and expense, upper limit, split savings

Incorporating features of both value- and cost-based contracts, this method rewards the consultant for keeping costs down.

The client agrees to pay for all the time put into a project at negotiated hourly billing rates. These rates include labor, overhead, and profit. The consultant and client agree to an upper limit to the total fee to be paid. Should the total amount billed reach that upper limit, the consultant is responsible to cover all costs incurred beyond that point.

However, you should not accept risk without a comparable reward, so this contract type offers an incentive to keep costs below the preset limit. The difference between the total project fees and the preset limit will be split, 50/50 between the consultant and the client.

For example, the consultant and client agree to hourly billing rates and an upper limit of $45,000. Throughout the project the consultant has worked hard to keep costs under control. When the project is complete, the consultant has invoiced the client a total of $38,500 which, under the hourly billing rates, pays labor, overhead, and profit. The difference between the total billed and the upper limit, $6,500, is split with the consultant who is paid an additional $3,250 in incentive compensation.

The obvious advantage of this arrangement is the incentive for the consultant to work in the best interest of the client. The client wins by having a preestablished upper limit to costs. The disadvantage is that the consultant may be tempted to cut corners and do less in order to keep costs down. Additionally, if the project was poorly scoped, it could result in costs which exceed the upper limit.

Summary of Time and Expense, Upper Limit, Split Savings

advantage	Strong incentive to work in the client's best interest
advantage	Client knows costs ahead of time
advantage	Firm has guaranteed profit in hourly billing rates
advantage	Firm stands to earn additional incentive profit
disadvantage	Temptation to cut corners
disadvantage	Costs could exceed upper limit

Cost-based contracts

Cost-based contracts determine the consultant's fee based on a multiplier of the cost incurred in delivering the project. While risk is minimized since the client generally agrees to cover all costs, reward is also limited since profit can never exceed the predetermined multiplier which the consultant has been able to negotiate.

Regardless of the ultimate contract type, virtually all fees are, at least initially, calculated on the basis of the cost to do the work. Obviously this is only good business practice if a firm has some notion of the costs it will incur to deliver the work. But while value-based and middle-of-the-road contracts use cost data as a point of departure from which different compensation methods are determined, cost-based contracts use this as the sole means of establishing fees.

Cost-based, time and expense contract

In a time and expense contract, the client agrees to pay the firm, at predetermined hourly billing rates, for all hours invested in the project. In addition, they agree to reimburse the firm for any direct project expenses incurred. While an estimate of total fees will likely be prepared, there is no preset limit on the amount of time the firm will spend on the project.

The obvious advantage of this contract type is its inherent safety. The consultant will be paid for each hour invested and the billing rates cover all costs and include a profit.

There are some obvious disadvantages of this contract as well. The most visible is the client's exposure to an open-ended billing scheme with no assurance the work will be complete within anything like a reasonable budget. Few clients are prepared to accept this risk. The other, less obvious disadvantage is to the consultant. When a contract is based on an hourly billing rate, the firm will bill only for those hours spent on the project. The profit percentage built into the charge for each hour is the maximum profit the firm can make. Regardless of how hard or efficiently the firm works, they can never exceed this percentage.

Like some of the middle-of-the-road contracts discussed earlier, the consultant is faced with a dilemma on a time and expense job. If the firm is working in the client's best interest, the firm will do its utmost to get the job done as quickly as possible. The reward for this effort? Lower revenue and lower profit. The only way the firm can increase revenue and profit is to expend more hours on the job which is decidedly not in the client's interest.

Despite these weaknesses, this contract type is often a firm's only option when the scope of a project is either unknown or poorly defined. It is often used in the early stages of a project when the consultant is helping the client define a proper scope. Once the project is well-defined and a detailed task list can be prepared, both the consultant and the client will be better off switching to a value-based or middle-of-the-road contract.

Summary of Time and Expense Contract

advantage	necessary when scope is poorly defined
advantage	no risk of loss and profit is assured with each hour of billing
advantage	client can control costs by calling halt to project at any time
disadvantage	percentage of profit is preset and consultant has no ability to increase profit
disadvantage	conflict with client's best interests

"Why-don't-you-just-shoot-me-now" contracts

These contract types are, for the most part, entirely in one party's favor and offer no advantage to the other. They are classic, "win-lose" arrangements and have no part in the strong, relationship-basis of design contracts. Historically, most of these win-lose agreements weigh heavily in the client's favor although it is not unheard of to find an architect or engineer who takes unfair advantage of a client with an inappropriate contract.

While most contract types have a balance of risk and reward factors on both sides of the table, these contracts shift all the risk to one party and all the reward to the other. Why would someone sign such a deal? Several factors are influential. First, design consultants tend to have fewer "bargaining table skills" than many of their business-oriented clients. Second, on a project for which many firms are competing, the client can easily terminate negotiations with a firm that is "bargaining too hard," and begin discussions with another firm saying, "every other firm will sign it!" Finally, many principals and project managers need to increase their understanding of the implications of the various contract types available to them.

"Why-don't-you-just-shoot-me-now", time and expense to a maximum contracts

This contract type takes the cost-based format of time and expense, but adds a preset, finite cap beyond which the client will not pay any more. With this arrangement, the consultant has all the disadvantages of the time and expense contract - a preset profit percentage which cannot be increased and a conflict with client's best interests. However, if the scope doesn't change and the costs hit the preestablished limit, the contract converts to a lump sum basis in which the firm is responsible for costs in excess of the fee.

There is no way a firm can win with this contract, yet many client agencies, particularly in the public sector, have been using this format for many years. The high incidence of this contract type is a sure indicator of intense competition for projects and a poor ability to negotiate win-win outcomes.

Smart firms, when asked to sign this contract type will often agree to a lump sum agreement with a lower total cost instead. For example, if the client offers a time and expense to a maximum contract, the firm may suggest it will accept the contract, with a fee cap of $50,000. However, if the client agrees to a lump sum contract, the lump sum will be a more reasonable, $45,000. These firms would prefer the risk/reward balance of the value-based contract to the higher limit of the one-sided deal.

Summary of Time and Expense to a Maximum

advantage	None to the consultant
advantage	All to the client
disadvantage	Percentage of profit is preset and consultant has no ability to increase profit
disadvantage	All the risks of a Lump Sum contract with none of the rewards

"Why-don't-you-just-shoot-me-now" lump sum with a vague scope of work contract

The only contract type worse than the time and expense to a maximum is a lump sum or fixed fee contract with a vague or poorly defined scope of work. A contract of this sort asks the engineer or architect to guarantee a price before the work to be done has been determined. This is the equivalent of negotiating a price on the car lot, then, after the price has been established, having the dealer tell you the kind of car and options you will get for the price you have negotiated!

Obviously, this is a ludicrous notion. Yet, many firms regularly find themselves in this situation. Prior to signing any contract, you must be able to determine the scope of work. If it's impossible to establish, or, if part of the scope of work is to establish a clearly defined set of tasks to be accomplished, choose an appropriate contract type which will not expose you to such high risks.

Summary of Lump Sum with a Vague Scope Of Work

advantage	None to the consultant
advantage	All to the client
disadvantage	Extremely high risk since the extent and cost of the work are unknown

Mixing and changing contract types

There is no requirement that says you must have a single contract type which covers the entire project. In fact, there are many advantages to varying the type of contract under which you are working throughout the various stages of the job.

In the earliest segments of the work, it is not uncommon for the scope of work to be undefined. Programming and schematic design often lead to fundamental changes in the way a client thinks about a project. It is also at these stages that the strength of your ideas represent the greatest value whether they were spawned in five weeks or five minutes. These situations present conflicting contract demands. On the one hand, an ill-defined scope suggests a cost-based, hourly contract in these early stages. On the other hand, an hourly contract might drastically discount the value of your creative ideas and the "big picture" solutions you offer the client.

In these situations, you must evaluate the risk/reward mix. You may discover it's best to opt for a middle-of-the-road contract in the early design stages.

As the project progresses and you enter the documentation phase, it is common, by then, that the scope has been thoroughly defined and you can assemble a detailed task list. From this it should be no problem to compile a time and cost estimate. This phase, however, is also the time when aggressive and skilled project management can result in significant time savings on the job. With a lump sum agreement in place for this portion of the work, you can save the client time, guarantee a fixed fee and reward your good management skills with additional profits.

In the construction phases of most projects, the demands on an engineer's or architect's time for site review are difficult to predict. Given the sometimes unpredictable nature of construction activity, it's highly likely you will be called upon for services beyond those you may have defined. The on-call nature of this work and the necessity of being available when the contractor needs you, also makes it difficult to accurately predict the time and cost demands. For these reasons, construction administration services are often contracted under a strict time and expense agreement.

Even the most traditional design-bid-build type jobs are essentially three separate projects in one. The first is the design work which is often vaguely defined and difficult to predict. The second is the documentation work which ought to be scheduled and budgeted with great accuracy. And finally, the construction work, which is largely an "on-call" arrangement.

Don't assume a single contract will be suitable for the entire job. Mix and match your contract types to suit the work at hand.

Choosing the right contract

When choosing or recommending a contract structure, there are two factors to consider. The first, and most important, is always:

What is the most appropriate contract type for the services to be provided?

The primary criteria for this decision is the degree to which the project and its tasks are defined and quantifiable. If the task is open-ended or the client has not clearly defined the problem to be solved, a cost-based contract is your only option.

Even when a project has not yet been defined, clients will frequently attempt to pressure you into establishing limits on total costs. While it's only natural that they work to protect their interests, don't overly compromise your own. If there are risks to be taken on the project, they should be shared. The client should not be asked to sign on to an open-ended deal with vague deliverables. Nor should you be asked to commit to a price or schedule before you know the tasks to be done.

The second factor to consider in choosing a contract type is:

What is the most advantageous contract type for this project?

While numerous contract types may work, which one offers the features and risk/reward balances that bring the greatest advantage to you and your client? Several criteria should be considered.

1. Who has control over the project outcome?

   If the firm has a significant ability to influence the outcome of the project - by reducing schedule or costs or increasing client profit performance, for example - a value-based contract is more advantageous.

2. How is your expertise being used?

   If you are being retained primarily as a "technician," that is, to perform relatively straightforward work which could be accomplished by many firms, such as producing a set of standard contract documents, you may want to consider a middle-of-the-road deal which has moderate risk and reward. The effort will require a predictable time investment, but can benefit from efficient project management. The work will not likely benefit from high levels of creativity, but rather from an efficient production process. In this case, the middle-of-the-road contract will compensate the time invested and provide incentives for increased productivity.

If, on the other hand, your work has a high creativity component, you want to be compensated for the value of your ideas, not the time necessary to uncover them. Here you may want to use a value-based, incentive contract.

3. Are your goals and your client's goals compatible?

If your client is driven to keep costs as low as possible, select a contract type which rewards you for saving money. If, on the other hand, they have a specific process which must be followed, don't establish a contract which penalizes you for the time needed to comply with their requirements.

Progress Review: Part 5

Check either True or False in response to each of the following statements.

True	False	
❒	❒	1. Value-based contracts provide the consultant with the best opportunity to balance profit incentive with client service.
❒	❒	2. Each contract type represents a different balance between risk and reward.
❒	❒	3. Percentage-of-construction provides a strong incentive to work in the client's best interest.
❒	❒	4. Splitting cost savings with a client provides a classic win-win situation.
❒	❒	5. Consultants should always use a time and expense contract because it offers the least risk.
❒	❒	6. Time and expense to a maximum is popular because it is fair to both parties.
❒	❒	7. Cost-plus-fixed-fee sets limits on the actual dollar amount a consultant can realize.
❒	❒	8. You should always set and keep a single contract type through the duration of any project.
❒	❒	9. Entrepreneurial consultants and clients are often attracted to incentive-based contracts.
❒	❒	10. The manner in which your expertise is being used can significantly affect the type of contract you should use.

Score your responses

1. - T 2. - T 3. - F 4. - T 5. - F
6. - F 7. - T 8. - F 9. - T 10. - T

9 - 10	Great	We can trust you to make the right choices regarding contract types for your projects.
7 - 8	Good	Don't sign a contract until you've reviewed this chapter again.
0 - 6	Poor	Better let someone else review the contracts you sign.

Invoices, accounts receivable and collections

It's your money! What's it doing in their bank?

Chapter 6

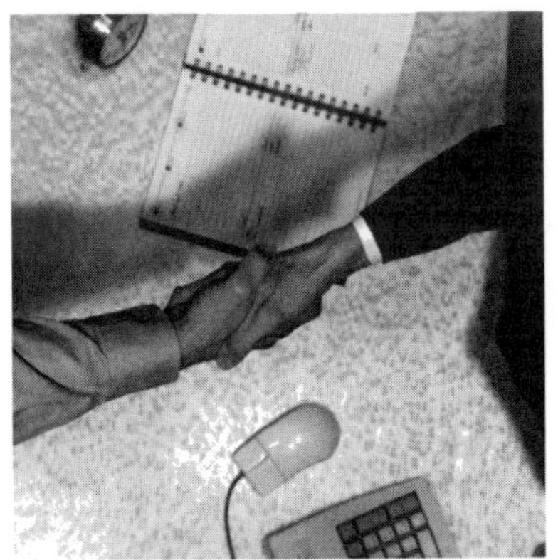

Introduction

You work hard to win and produce projects in your firm. So there's little that is more annoying and even insulting than a client that refuses to pay your bill.

There are, no doubt, circumstances under which payment might be legitimately delayed. In these situations, where your client has justifiable concerns about quality, performance, or errors in billing, you must act quickly to remove any and all concerns to keep the client happy.

But what should you do when the client simply refuses to pay or promises to pay but fails to come through with a check? As with many of life's problems, solving the problem is often a case of avoiding it in the first place.

Actions during contract negotiations

Effective collection of accounts receivable will always begin long before your first invoice is sent. During your contract negotiations, many issues regarding payment terms and conditions should be addressed and agreed upon. Follow these steps to cover any possible loopholes and head off many of the classic stalling tactics.

- Be sure the terms of payment are included in your contract with the client. These terms should include the frequency at which invoices will be sent, whether weekly, bi-weekly, monthly, or at specific project milestones. If invoicing is to take place monthly, specify the time of the month when your bill will be sent. The clause might look something like:

"Invoices for work on the project will be sent once a month for services performed during the previous billing period. The invoice will be mailed no later than the last day of every month and payment is due on receipt of the invoice. Should there be any questions regarding the invoice, the project manager will be contacted by the client within five working days of receipt of the invoice. Should the Project Manager not be contacted regarding the invoice in this time, it will be taken as confirmation that the invoice is acceptable to the client and duly payable in accordance with these terms."

- Inquire about the client's payment cycle to determine the best time of the month to submit your invoice. If the client's organization processes bills and writes checks on the 20th of every month, for example, you should find out when the invoice must be in to be included in the month's payment cycle.
- If you normally bill monthly, consider increasing your billing cycle to bi-weekly. The increased cash flow from smaller, but more regular payments will help level out the monthly ups and downs of your bank balance.
- Include interest charges for late payments as a term in your contract. Then, when payments are late, issue a statement to which interest charges have been added. All clients may not actually pay the charges, but their presence on a statement adds a subtle pres-

sure to pay the bill. Also, should the unpaid amount end up going to litigation or arbitration, you are much more likely to collect the additional amount as payment for your inconvenience.

- Always ask for a retainer on all projects. While many firms insist on a retainer from new clients, few ask for one from existing clients. This is generally seen as a statement of trust and courtesy, which is true. However, it doesn't change the fact that those clients are using your money to finance their project for 30 or 60 days as you wait for payment. All attorneys ask their clients for retainers and work against a block of your money sitting in their account. They even specify that the retainer cannot fall below a predetermined amount or they will stop work on your case. How do attorneys get a retainer? They ask for it. You can be sure that if you don't ask, the client will never volunteer to pay you money up front.
- Include the specific action steps to be taken in case of nonpayment as a clause in your contract. This should include your option of stopping work on the project. The clause might look something like:

"Invoices that remain unpaid after 60 days from the date of the invoice will cause all work on the project to cease. If payment has not been received after 75 days from the date of the invoice, a lien will be filed on the project. The client will be liable for all reasonable collection costs and legal fees."

- Include the format of your invoice as a topic of discussion during the negotiations. Determine ahead of time the precise information the client wants to be included in the invoice and in what format it should be rendered. Sort out the invoice format before billing begins, not when you're in the midst of trying to collect an overdue bill. Attach a sample copy of your invoice format, initialed by the client, to your contract as an exhibit.

Actions during the project

There is an old saying among design professionals: "Happy clients pay their bills." You can significantly aid your collections process by working to keep that client as happy as possible.

The number one way to keep a client happy is through frequent and regular communication. Make it a habit to call every active client at least once a week for the sole purpose of updating. You may have spoken yesterday but the conversation was likely about a specific issue. If clients know they can count on you for strong, proactive communication, their confidence will be high and they will feel good about signing off on your invoice.

If, on the other hand, they never hear from you until they get the bill, they will find many things to question about your invoice and many excuses to delay payment. Your silence breeds their suspicion.

Actions at billing time

There are a number of specific tactics you can use as you prepare your invoices which will speed up payments or, at the very least, remove many of the common excuses for delayed payments.

- Get your invoices out regularly and on time. If you've negotiated to invoice by the tenth of every month for the previous month's work, get the bills out on time. How can you expect the client to honor a payment schedule if you can't stick to your billing schedule?
- Provide all information and backup that you know will be necessary along with the invoice. It's an old trick to delay payments by asking for backup on the invoice.
- Submit separate invoices for professional fees and reimbursable expenses. If you include both categories on one bill and there is a disagreement over an expense item, or a request for further information or backup, it will hold up payment for the larger fee amount. Separate invoices remove any reason to hold up payment on the bill which is not being questioned.
- Confirm the person, department, and correct address for billings. Sending an invoice to the wrong person or department can delay payment for weeks.
- If invoices must be reviewed and approved by several individuals within the client's organization, print multiple copies of the invoices, send the original to the correct department, and send a copy stamped "Copy-For Review" in red to everyone who must approve it. By the time the original is circulated to their desk, they will already have seen and reviewed the invoice and it will cut down on the time your bill sits in their "In" basket.

Actions after the bill has been sent

- Call the client five days after the invoice is mailed to check if the client has actually received the invoice. The number one excuse for delayed payment is, "I never received it, please send it again."

- During that call, ask if the client has any questions or concerns regarding the invoice. The number two excuse for delayed payment is, "I'm glad you called (now that the invoice is 30 days old!) because I have some problems with this bill that we need to discuss." By calling after five days, you remove the top two reasons for delayed payments.

- If any amount is past due at the time of this billing, send a monthly statement showing the status of the client's account. Be sure to add the interest charges which you included in your contract. This keeps the issue front and center and lets the client know that prompt payment is important to you.

Actions when payment is overdue

All your great service, subtle hints, and contract clauses won't always get the invoice paid. If the check still isn't forthcoming, it's time to initiate more drastic measures.

Step 1 When the invoice is 10 days overdue.

Accounting staff should make a polite "reminder" call on the assumption the invoice has simply been forgotten. This will often clear the matter and no further action is needed.

If, however, the account is obviously overdue and problematic, all collection activity from this point forward should be handled by the project manager or the principal in charge. This signals the client regarding the level at which these matters will be handled. While it's fine to have accounting staff make the initial "reminder" call, serious receivables must be handled at the management level. This also allows you to diplomatically collect the outstanding amount while still preserving the relationship.

Step 2 When the invoice is 20 days overdue.

Call the client and specifically ask if there is a problem with your services. Tell them you have heard no reports of any problems which should delay payment and if there are, you certainly want to hear about them. Tell the client how much you want this project to succeed and how you appreciate their cooperation by making timely payments. Ask the client when you can expect to receive their check.

Step 3 When the invoice is 30 days overdue.

If they refuse to commit, or if a check does not arrive within two days of the promised date, call again and request a personal meeting to discuss the problem. At this point in the discussion you should offer to send a courier to pick up the check. Don't allow any more "it's in the mail" delays.

Step 4 When the invoice is 45 days overdue.

It's time to put things in writing. Your letter should state your "serious concern" regarding the outstanding account. Review the steps you have taken to collect so far and any payment promises the client has made. Be sure to note that you have heard no suggestions that your services were unsatisfactory. Issue a velvet-covered threat by offering to "slow down or pause the work if cash flow is a temporary problem" for the client.

Step 5 When the invoice is 60 days overdue.

Slow the pace of the work on the project considerably, but do not stop. Do not respond to inquiries from the client and issue no progress prints or reports. Send a sternly-worded letter stating that all work is about to cease and the issue will be handed over to legal counsel for collections.

Step 6 When the invoice is 75 days overdue.

Stop all work on the project and have your attorney send a letter of intention to lien the project.

Step 7 When the invoice is 90 days overdue

File a lien and prepare for a court battle.

Some general tips for collections

- Don't hesitate to ask persistently for your money. Many firms use the excuse that, "I don't want to offend them," or "they might get mad and not hire us again." Both these statements are excuses to avoid the confrontation of collections. First, if they take offense at being asked to stick to the terms of the contract they have signed and pay you the money they owe you, this is not a client you want to be working with. Second, if you're afraid they might not hire you again, consider this: You wanted them to hire you so they would pay you. They are not paying you. Do you want to be hired so they won't pay you again?
- Some clients are happy to use you as a bank to finance their project. If they hold your money for an additional 30 or 60 days, you must pay interest on your line of credit to meet your obligations in the interim, and they get free use of your funds.
- If you intend to have a long-term relationship with the client and fail to establish the terms of that relationship at the outset, you will never be able to recover from the initial habit of late payment. In addition, the client's respect for you as a person of business will fall dramatically.
- Throughout the entire collections effort, maintain a positive demeanor while remaining firm. Let your guiding mood be firm, fair, and friendly.
- Let them know you have obligations to pay and require their payment in order to meet those obligations. Consultants who have worked on their project are also waiting for their money and you don't want to jeopardize the project or your relationship with them by not paying on time.
- Never offer a discount or change the payment terms as an inducement to pay. If you discount the invoice, the client will only learn that, if they delay payment long enough, you will lower the price.

- Don't threaten any action which you are not prepared to follow through on. If you threaten to lien the project if payment has not been received by a deadline, do it.
- Maintain a written record of everything that happens during your collections effort. Keep copies of invoices, statements which were sent, notes on telephone calls and dates when messages were left, etc. If the issue does end up in court, your documentation will go a long way towards receiving your money.

Progress Review: Part 6

Check either True or False in response to each of the following statements.

True	False	
❒	❒	1. The best time to institute reliable collections is before the first invoice is ever mailed.
❒	❒	2. It's a good idea to include your terms of payment and a copy of your standard invoice as an attachment to the contract.
❒	❒	3. Increasing your billing frequency will have no impact on your cash flow.
❒	❒	4. Asking for a retainer from existing clients is considered bad business practice.
❒	❒	5. You can make collections easier by maintaining weekly contact with all your clients whether there is something specific to discuss or not.
❒	❒	6. You should always combine professional fees with reimbursable expenses in the same invoice.
❒	❒	7. Don't take any action on an overdue invoice until it is at least 30 days past due.
❒	❒	8. It's important to establish positive and regular payment terms to maintain long term client relationships.
❒	❒	9. Never offer a discount or change payment terms as an inducement for a client to pay.
❒	❒	10. You can often get a client to pay if you threaten a lawsuit, even if you have no intention of following through on the threat.

Score your responses

1. - T 2. - T 3. - F 4. - F 5. - T
6. - F 7. - F 8. - T 9. - T 10. - F

9 - 10	Great	You should not have too many problems with overdue receivables.
7 - 8	Good	You should review these again or you may find yourself struggling to collect money that belongs to you.
0 - 6	Poor	This isn't a non-profit charity organization! You need to go back and study this section again.

About the Author

David Stone is a senior consultant for FMI, management consultants to the construction industry. A member of the firm's Engineering & Architectural Services Group, he works with design professionals in the areas of marketing, business development, and project management.

Trained as an architect, David spent 15 years as a practicing design professional. Since 1989, he has been a highly respected and sought-after consultant, speaker, and author. His remarkable ability to quickly develop innovative and successful business strategies is regularly called upon by top executives of the most prominent design companies. Using highly developed facilitation skills, he regularly works at the highest corporate levels to build consensus on strategic and tactical business initiatives.

David's proposal writing methods have reinvented the way design firms pursue large projects. He has developed and taught rapid-fire techniques to identify and exploit pivotal success hot buttons in individual sales efforts and regularly directs corporate proposal, presentation, and sales efforts for the largest and most important projects.

With a rare ability to speak powerfully and articulately, David's energy and enthusiasm regularly captivate audiences at state, national, and international gatherings of engineers and architects throughout the United States, Canada, and Australia.

As a writer, David is both talented and prolific. His many books include *Mastering the Business of Design*, *The Art & Science of Pricing*, *The Ultimate Project Management Manual*, *Winning Proposals*, *Wired: How to crawl inside your client's head for success in business development*, and *Selling Design Services.*

About FMI

Founded in 1953 by Dr. Emol A. Fails, FMI provides management consulting, training, and capital services for the worldwide construction industry.

FMI delivers innovative, customized solutions to contractors; engineers, architects; manufacturers and suppliers of building materials and construction equipment; construction materials producers; facility owners, managers, and developers; surety companies; industry trade associations.

FMI's experienced consultants assist businesses with strategic planning, leader and organizational development, marketing and sales, compensation planning, strategic market information, mergers and acquisitions, acquisition integration, private equity financing, project partnering and teambuilding, and management and field-level training.